LESSON 1

A Point, say and write

1 Alan's washing his hands.
2 ....
3 ....
4 ....
5 ....

B Look and write

1 What's he doing?   He's writing a letter.
2 ....
3 ....
4 ....
5 ....

one 1

C Choose and write

You've got a cut.   Here's an ice cream.
You've got a bump. Oh dear. Poor Rover.

LESSON 2

A Look and write

Is she skipping?

1   No, she isn't. She's running.

Is he reading?

2   ....

Is he singing?

3   ....

Is she writing?

4   ....

B Look and write   What are you doing?

I'm reading.

C Look and write

Lucy: Have you got a pen?
Max: Yes, ...I have........ .

Lucy: Have you got a rubber?

Max: No, ...

Lucy: Have .... a ruler?

Max: .... Have you got a calculator?

Lucy: No, ... Have .... a pencil?

Max: .... Have you got a pencil?

Lucy: ....

LESSON 3

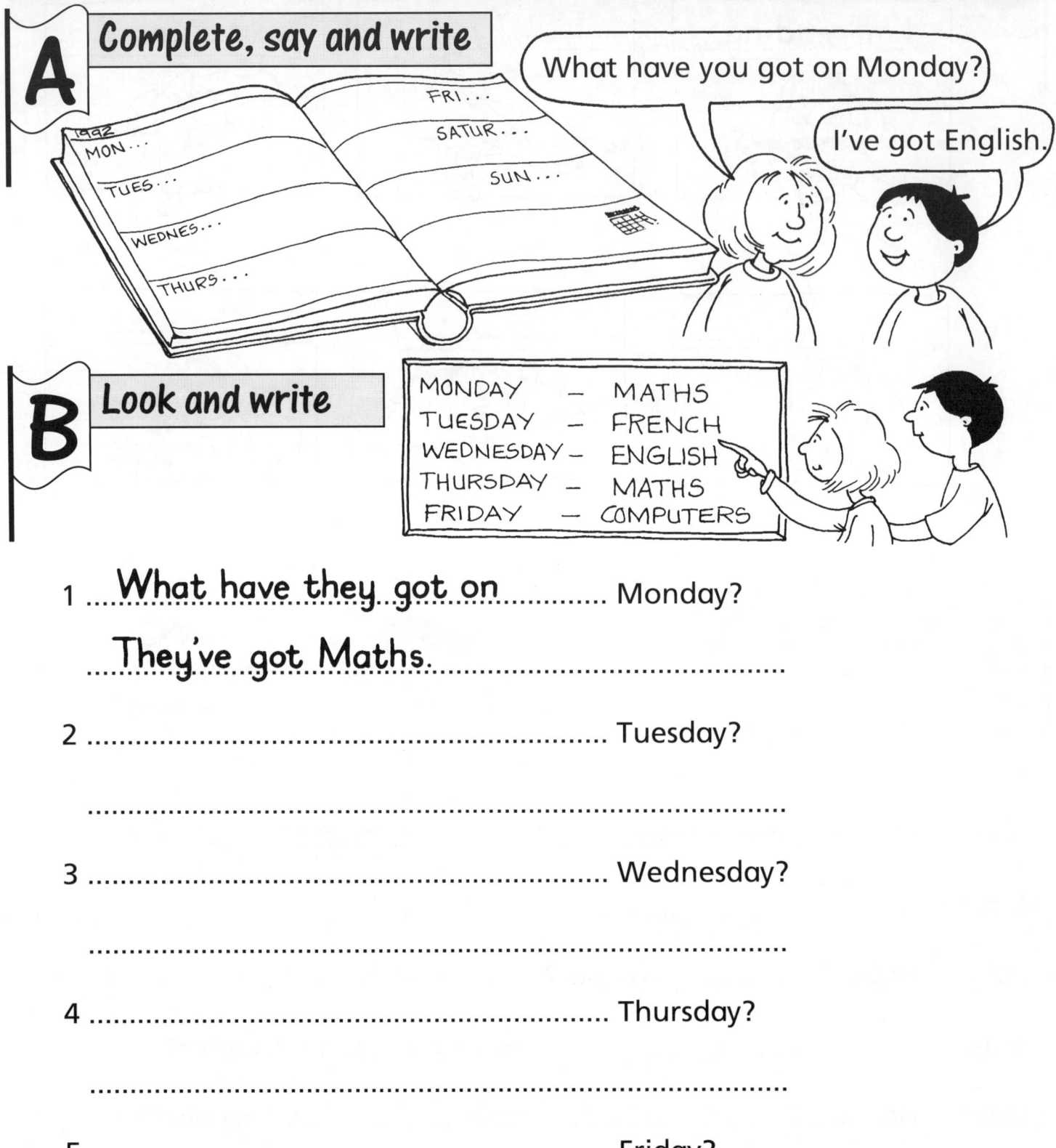

1. What have they got on Monday?
   They've got Maths.

2. .... Tuesday?
   ....

3. .... Wednesday?
   ....

4. .... Thursday?
   ....

5. .... Friday?
   ....

C Draw and write

long   short   big   small   hair   eyes   nose   mouth   ears

Write about your partner.   Draw your partner.

.............'s got..

....

....

....

LESSON 4

A Point, say and write

Today is Monday.

1 They're feeding the crocodiles at three o'clock.

2 ....monkeys....................................

3 ....lions..

4 ....penguins..................................

five 5

B Write

What's the time?

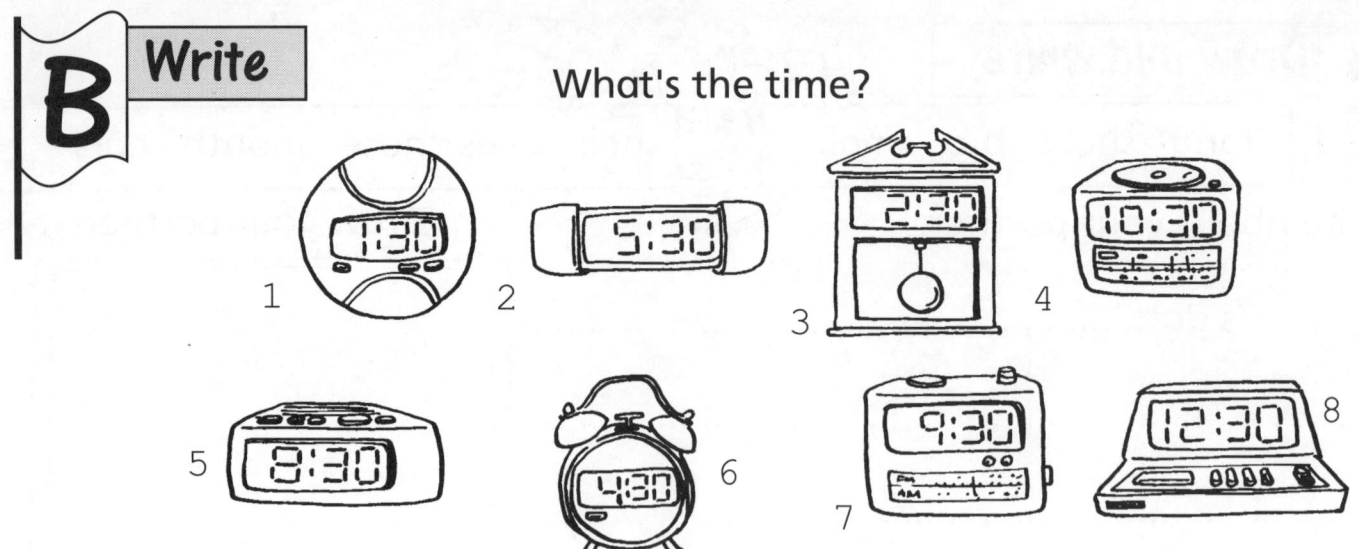

1 It's half past one.
2 ....
3 ....
4 ....
5 ....
6 ....
7 ....
8 ....

C Find and write

1 15
2 30
3 14
4 50
5 13 .... fifteen ....
6 40

LESSON 5

A. Listen and write

MONDAY	Maths	9:00
TUESDAY	....	....
WEDNESDAY	....	....
THURSDAY	....	....
FRIDAY	....	....

B. Listen and circle

1 (Ten) / Two   table tennis tables on   Tuesday. / Thursday.

2 Five / Fifteen   footballs on   Friday. / Monday.

C. Say and write

1. a triangle   2. ....   3. ....   4. ....

5. ....   6. ....   7. ....   8. ....

seven 7

LESSON 6

Find and write

- a book ✓

LESSON 7

A Point, say and write

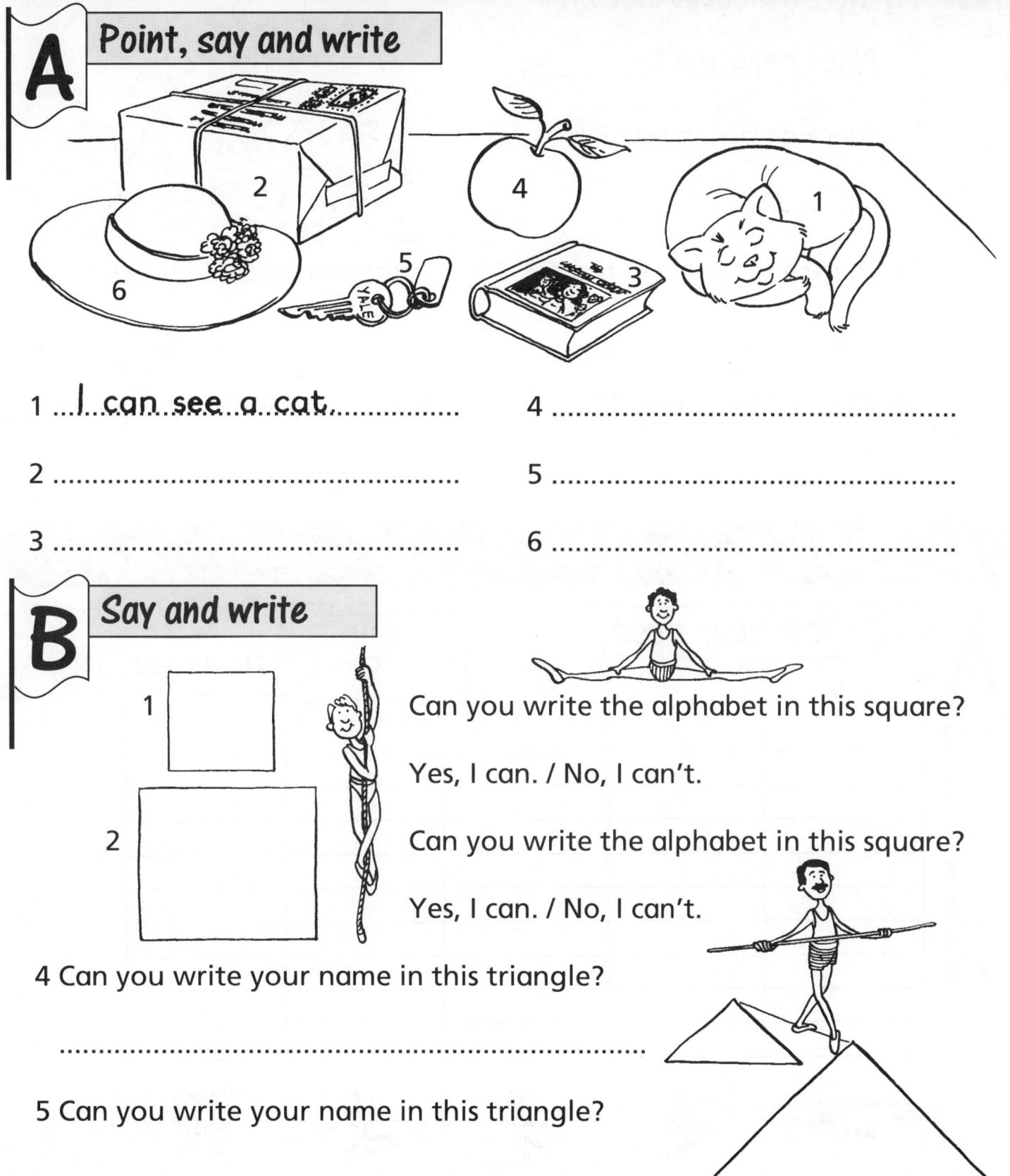

1 ...I can see a cat................. 4 ....

2 .... 5 ....

3 .... 6 ....

B Say and write

Can you write the alphabet in this square?

Yes, I can. / No, I can't.

Can you write the alphabet in this square?

Yes, I can. / No, I can't.

4 Can you write your name in this triangle?

....

5 Can you write your name in this triangle?

....

nine 9

C Look and write

1 Is there a monkey in row 2?

No, there isn't.

2 Is there an owl in row 3?

....

3 Is there a crocodile in row 5?

....

4 Is there a lion in row 3?

....

5 Is there a rabbit in row 5?

....

6 Is there a penguin in row 4?

....

LESSON 8

A Ask about your class

Can you ....?
Yes, I can. ✓   No, I can't. ✗

B Write about your class

Look at Section A.

How many children can ....?

1 ....
2 ....
3 ....
4 ....
5 ....

C Choose and write

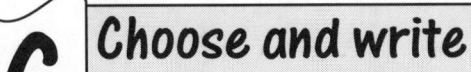

1 The monkey's ....behind the blackboard..

2 The lion's ....

3 The ant's ....

4 The penguin's ....

5 The cat's..

6 The elephant's..

LESSON 9

A Complete and write

Write the names in 1, 2, 3 and 4

1   Who is sitting in front of you?   ....

2   Who is sitting behind you?   ....

3   Who is sitting next to you?   ....

B Match

1 She's bringing   French.

2 I'm playing   the window.

3 We're eating   football.

4 We're sitting near   the drinks.

5 They're speaking   chicken.

C Look and write

1 Who is in front of number 1? Number 4 is in front of number 1.

2 Who is behind number 1? ....

3 Who is near the goal? ....

4 Who is next to number 3? ....

5 Who is in front of number 9? ....

6 Who is next to number 10? ....

LESSON 10

A Point, say and write

1 Let's ride ⟶ a song. Let's ride our bikes.

2 Let's watch   a letter. ....

3 Let's read   a kite.   ....

4 Let's sing   our bikes. ....

5 Let's write   a book.   ....

6 Let's fly   TV.   ....

thirteen 13

B Look and write

1 ...Are they... singing?   ...Yes, they are...
2 .... swimming?   ....
3 .... reading?   ....
4 .... hopping?   ....
5 .... eating?   ....
6 .... dancing?   ....

C Look and write

LONDON

ATHENS

BUENOS AIRES

MELBOURNE

1 ...What's the time... in London?   ...It's half past two...
2 .... in Athens?   ....
3 .... in Buenos Aires?   ....
4 .... in Melbourne?   ....

LESSON 11

A Ask about your class

When is your birthday?

My birthday's in April.

	1	2	3	4	5	6	7	8	9	10
JANUARY										
FEBRUARY										
MARCH										
APRIL										
MAY										
JUNE										
JULY										
AUGUST										
SEPTEMBER										
OCTOBER										
NOVEMBER										
DECEMBER										

B Write about your class   Look at section A.

1 ....

2 ....

3 ....

4 ....

5 ....

When is your teacher's birthday?

It's ....

fifteen **15**

C Look and write

A

B

1 dogs ....In picture A there are two dogs.....
....In picture B there is one dog.....

2 cats ....

3 ants ....

4 frogs ....

LESSON 12

A Point, say and write

1 10 ten
2 21 ....
3 32 ....
4 54 ....
5 76 ....
6 87 ....
7 98 ....
8 100 ....

B Write

7 days = 1 week   4 weeks = 1 month   12 months = 1 year

1 There are ....twenty four...... months in two years.

2 There are .... days in five weeks.

3 There are .... weeks in four months.

4 There are .... weeks .... two months.

5 There are .... days .... two weeks.

C Find the words

1 Listen to the ....clock...............

2 There are sixty days in two ....

3 There are twelve months in one ....

4 There are seven days in one ....

5 There are sixty minutes in one ....

6 There are fourteen .... in two weeks.

seventeen 17

LESSON 13

A Listen and write

1. snake
2. ....
3. ....
4. ....
5. ....
6. ....

Write the 'z' words..... trees,

Write the 's' words..... snake

B Listen and write

1 Can you hear a splash or a buzz?

..........a buzz..........

2 Can you hear a hiss or a buzz?

....

3 Can you hear a splash or a hiss?

....

4 Can you hear trees or keys?

....

C Listen and write

Write the 'ee' and 'e' words.

green

1. feet
2. ....
3. ....

red

1. pen
2. ....
3. ....

LESSON 14

Find and write

Can you see ....

1 a mouse on a skateboard? ✓

2 a monkey flying a kite? ☐

3 a clown eating ice cream? ☐

4 a taxi on the table? ☐

5 a boy brushing his teeth? ☐

6 a cat singing a song? ☐

.... ☐

.... ☐

.... ☐

.... ☐

.... ☐

.... ☐

.... ☐

.... ☐

nineteen 19

LESSON 15

A **Ask your class** Do you like ......? Yes, I do = ☑ No, I don't = ☒
Ask ten children in your class.

	1	2	3	4	5	6	7	8	9	10
English										
Maths										
basket-ball										
football										
elephants										
snakes										
monkeys										
chicken										
chips										
pizza										

B **Write about your class** Look at Section A.

1 .... chips.

2 .... chicken.

3 .... pizza.

4 .... monkeys.

5 .... snakes.

6 .... elephants.

7 .... football.

8 .... basket-ball.

9 .... Maths.

10 .... English.

B Write

Yes = ✓   No = ✗

1 Does Pete like ice cream? ✓ Yes, he does.
2 Does Polly like ice cream? ✓ ....
3 Does Max like apples? ✓ ....
4 Does Rose like apples? ✗ ....
5 Does Crocky like red monkeys? ✓ ....
6 Does Crocky like fat cats? ✗ ....
7 Does Annie like blue bananas? ✓ ....
8 Does Bill like blue bananas? ✗ ....
9 Does Miss Electra like crocodiles? ✓ ....
10 Does Lucy like crocodiles? ✗ ....

C Colour and write

0 - 10 = red
11 - 20 = brown
21 - 30 = blue
31 - 40 = yellow

1 bikes   The bikes are yellow.
2 cars   ....
3 buses   ....
4 taxi   ....

LESSON 17

A Draw and write

Grandmother Grandfather Mother Father Brother Sister

B Look and write

1 What's his name?

His name's Jaime

2 Where does he come from?

He comes from Spain

3 What's her name?

....

4 Where does she come from?

....

5 What's his name?

....

6 Where does he come from?

....

twenty-three 23

C Look and write

What's he got in his bag?

What's she got in her bag?

1 He's got a book.
2 ....
3 ....
4 ....

5 She's got a cake.
6 ....
7 ....
8 ....

LESSON 18

A Point, say and write

swim   bark   eat fish   sing   eat meat

1 It's a frog. It swims.
2 ....
3 ....
4 ....
5 ....

24 twenty-four

B Look and write

1. Rose plays football.
2. ....
3. ....
4. ....
5. ....
6. ....
7. ....
8. ....

These people play football.
ROSE, PETE, BOB, POLLY, MAX, MARY, LUCY, TOM
These people play volleyball.

C Complete

January			
March			

1 When is your birthday? ....

2 When is your mother's birthday? ....

3 When is your brother's birthday? ....

4 When is your father's birthday? ....

5 When is your sister's birthday? ....

6 When is your grandmother's birthday? ....

twenty-five 25

LESSON 19

A Choose and write

Winter   Autumn   Summer   Spring

1 In ...Spring............... new leaves grow on trees.

2 In .... flowers grow.

3 In .... leaves turn brown. They fall.

4 In .... snowflakes fall.

B Choose and write

cold   hot   raining   windy

1 It's hot.   2 ....   3 ....   4 ....

5 Don't take your coat. It's hot. ....

6 Take your coat. ....

7 Take your umbrella. ....

8 Don't take your umbrella. ....

C Point, say and write

1 Can you write the seasons here?

2 Can you write the seasons here?

....

3 Can you write 1-10 here? →

....

LESSON 20

A Look and write

1 ....How many............ Wednesdays ....are there in........ March?

.....There are four Wednesdays in March...........................

2 ....Sundays .... February?

....

3 ....Tuesdays .... March?

....

twenty-seven **27**

B Look and write

1. fifty-three
2. ....
3. ....
4. ....
5. ....
6. ....
7. ....
8. ....
9. ....

C Read and write

Rose's brother has got short hair.

He's got big ears.

He's got a small mouth.

He's got a long nose.

He's got small eyes.

Write about the monster. ....

....

....

LESSON 21

A Listen, draw and write

1 Two red trees. 2 .... 3 ....

4 .... 5 .... 6 ....

B Listen, write and say

1 What are you doing?   I'm counting sheep. ....

2 What is she doing?   ....

3 What is he doing?   ....

4 What are they doing?   ....

C Listen and complete

a b c d e f g h i j k l m
n o p q r s t u v w x y z

twenty-nine 29

LESSON 22

Find and write

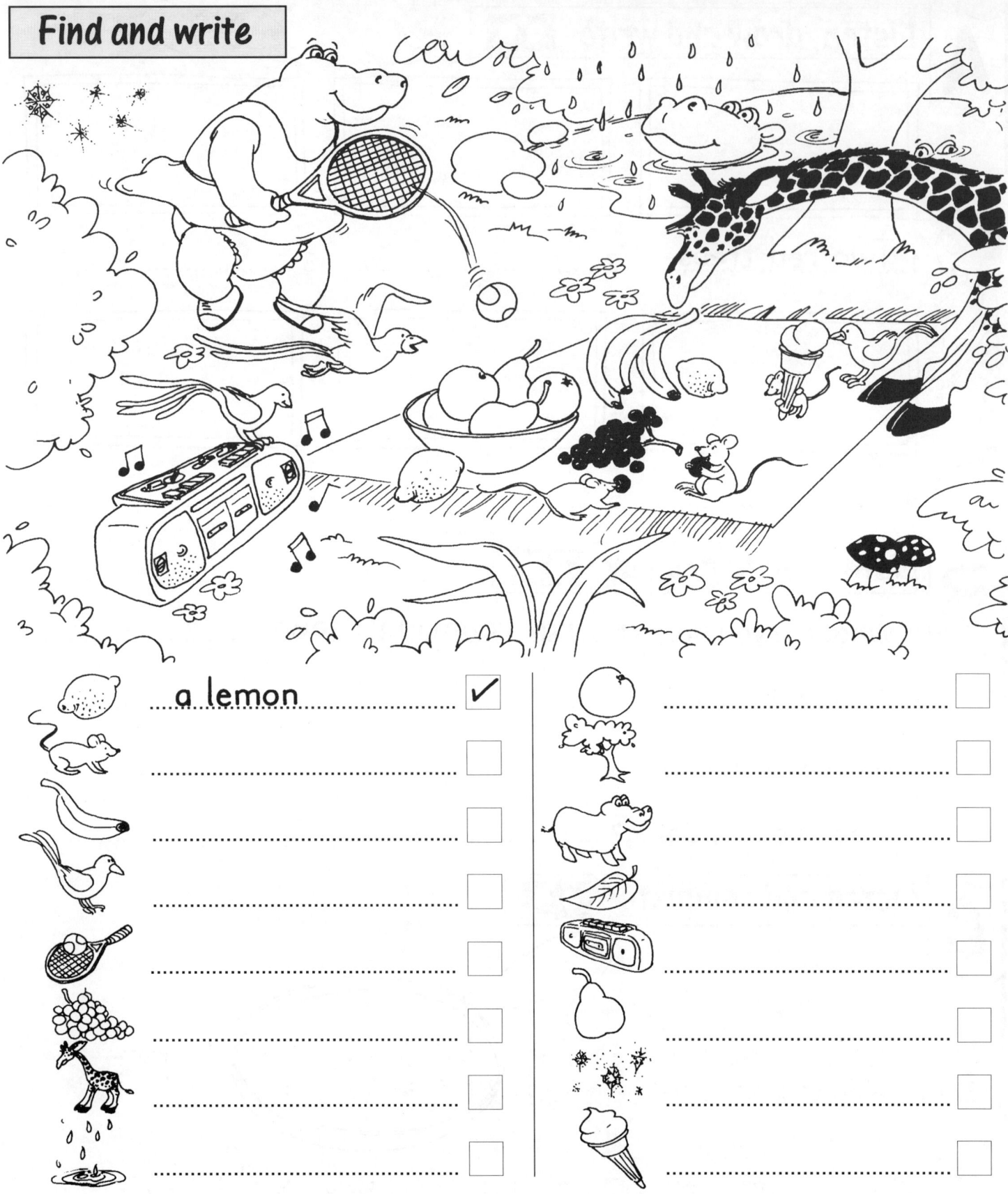

a lemon ✓

LESSON 23

A Point, say and write

1. ....Is she.......... reading a book?
   No, she isn't. She's making a cake.

2. .... eating a banana?
   ....

3. .... making a cake?
   ....

B Look and write

1. He's posting a letter.
2. ....
3. ....
4. ....

C Look and write

Look at Section B.

1 Who's sitting on a chair? Max

2 Who's posting a letter? ....

3 Who's watching TV? ....

4 Who's singing a song? ....

thirty-one 31

LESSON 24

A Match

1 I am — I'm
2 You are — You're
3 He is — He's
4 She is — She's
5 We are — We're
6 They are — They're

B Look and write

1 Is she sitting on a chair?
No, she isn't. She's sitting on a cat.

2 Is she making a kite?
....

3 Are they playing on a computer?
....

4 Are they sleeping in a chair?
....

5 Is she riding a bike?
....

C Look and write

1 Max ....likes pizza....................................
2 Max ....
3 Max ....
4 Rose ....
5 Rose ....
6 Rose ....
7 They ....
8 They ....

LESSON 25

A Point, say and write

Yes, you can. = ✓   No, you can't. = ✗

1 Can I try your pizza?
   Yes, you can.

2 ....
   ....

3 ....
   ....

B Look and write

1 In our cake there is a snake
2 ....
3 ....
4 ....
5 ....

C Look and write

This is a code.

0 1 2 3 4 5 6 7 8 9

1 What's this telephone number?

....

2 Write your telephone number in code.

....

3 Write your school's telephone number in code.

....

4 Write your partner's telephone number in code.

....

LESSON 26

A Find the words

crazy

....

....

....

....

....

B Look and write

1 The rabbit has got the fish's head.

2 ....

3 ....

4 ....

5 ....

6 ....

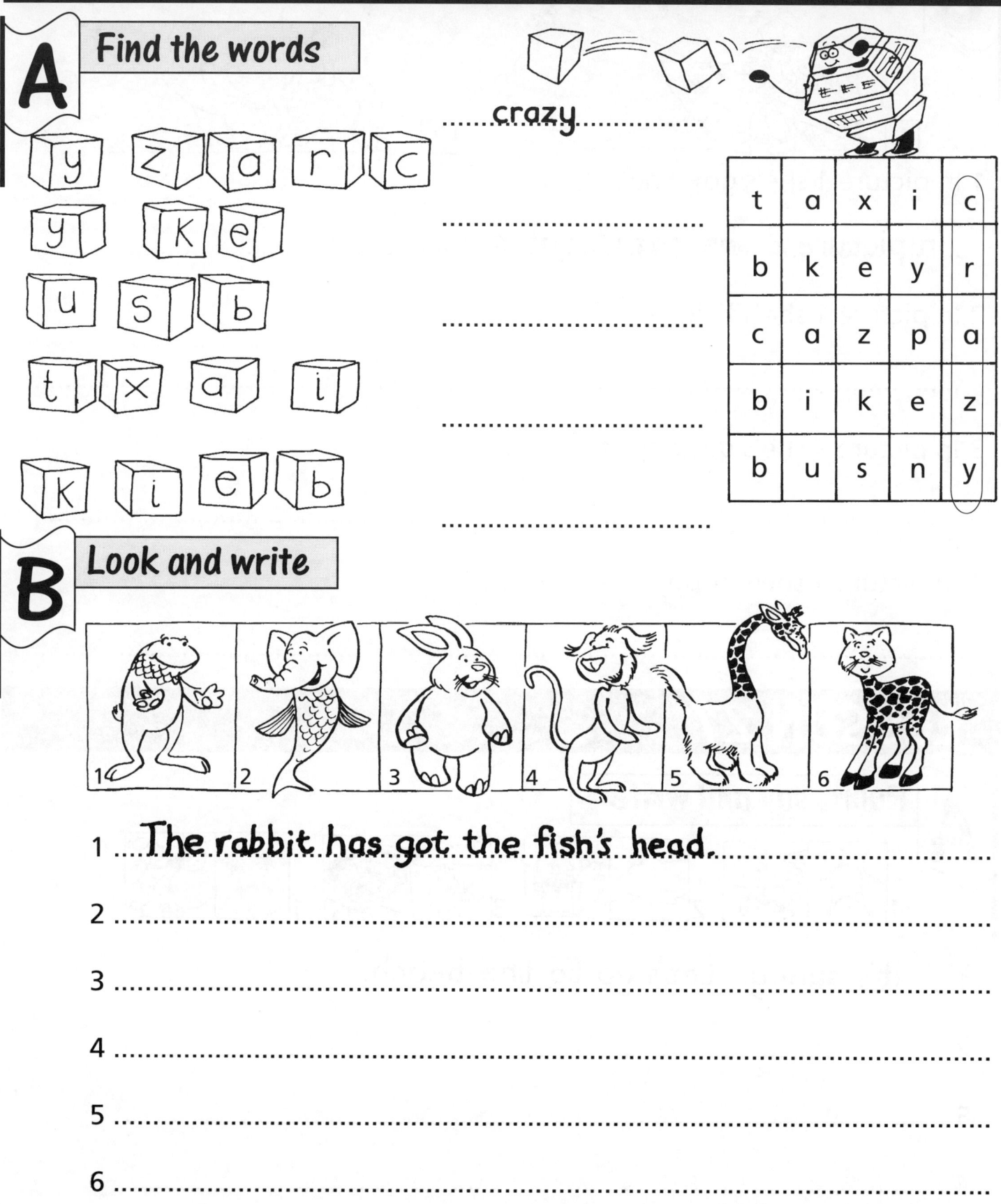

thirty-five 35

C Look and write

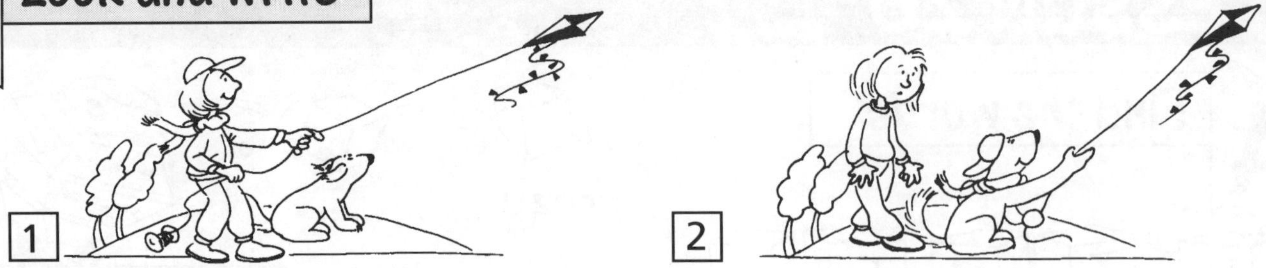

1 In picture 1 she's got a hat.

...In picture 2 she hasn't got a hat....................

2 In picture 1 she's flying a kite.

....

3 In picture 1 she's got a scarf.

....

4 In picture 1 she's happy.

....

LESSON 27

A Point, say and write

1 ...It's sunny. Let's go to the beach.........

2 ....

3 ....

4 ....

B Read, draw and write

1 This is Max.
   He's riding a bike.
   He's wearing a tracksuit.
   He's flying a kite.

2 This is Polly.
   She's riding a bike.
   She's wearing ski-boots and a scarf.
   She's got a bag.

3 This is ......Lucy............................

   She's riding ....

   She's wearing ....

   ....

   She's singing..................................

C Look and write

Yes = ☑   No = ☒

1 Are Bill and Andy sleeping? ☒ No, they aren't..........................

2 Are Bill and Annie talking? ☑ ....

3 Are Max and Rose running? ☒ ....

4 Are Max and Polly singing? ☑ ....

5 Are Rose and Rover eating? ☑ ....

thirty-seven 37

LESSON 28

A Point, say and write

1   get up   2   breakfast   3   dinner   4   bed

1 ......Max gets up at eight o'clock.................................
2 ....
3 ....
4 ....

B Draw and write

I get up at six o'clock.

1   get up   2   breakfast   3   lunch   4   dinner

1 ...I get up at.............................   3 ....
2 ....   4 ....

38 thirty-eight

C Look and write

1. ..Have you got.......... a pen?   ..Yes, I have...........................
2. .... rubber?   ....
3. .... ball?   ....
4. .... calculator? ....
5. .... orange?   ....

LESSON 29

A Listen and write
Write the 'a' and 'u' words.

c<u>a</u>t	s<u>u</u>n
1 ......can................	1 ......lunch..............
2	2 ....
3	3 ....
4	4 ....
5	5 ....

thirty-nine 39

B Listen and circle

Can I try your..........?

1 (hat) keypad
2 bike kite
3 calculator computer
4 scarf sock
5 skate skateboard
6 skis keys
7 shirt skirt

C Find, say and write

Catch the bus and go home.

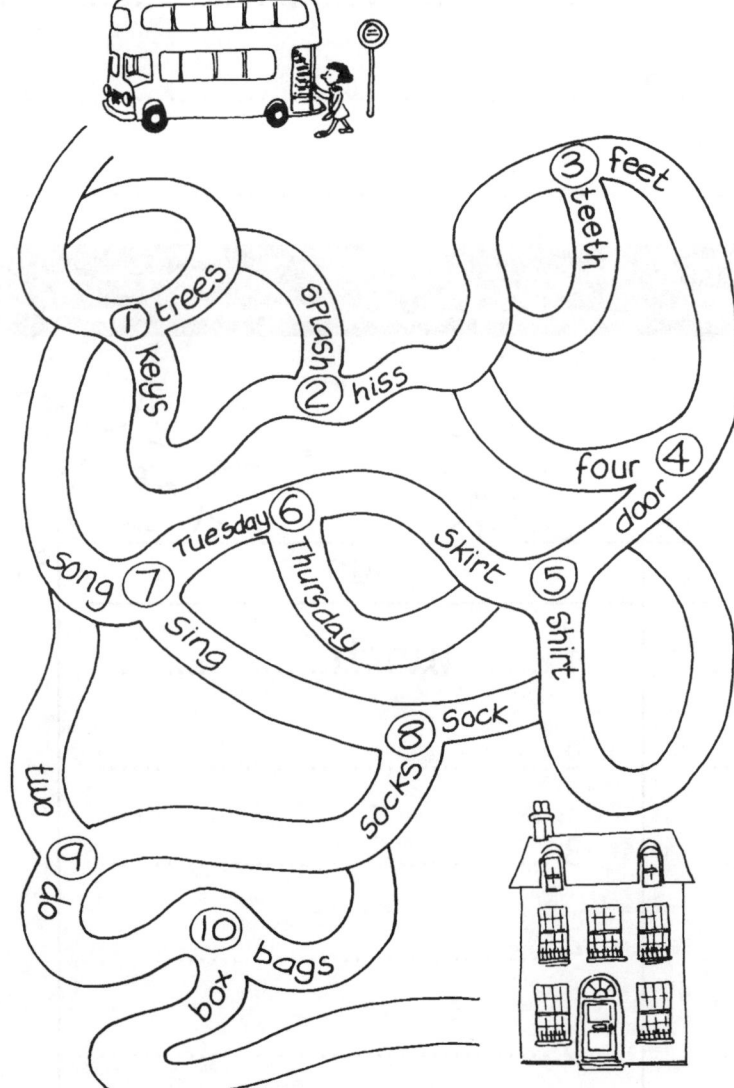

1 .keys.............................
2 ....
3 ....
4 ....
5 ....
6 ....
7 ....
8 ....
9 ....
10 ....

LESSON 30

Find and write

1 Can you see a cat? ☒   No, I can't.

2 Can you see a frog? ☐   ....

3 Can you see a snowman? ☐   ....

4 Can you see a piano? ☐   ....

5 Can you see a mouse? ☐   ....

6 Can you see a calculator? ☐   ....

7 How many people can you see?   ....

8 How many bananas can you see?   ....

9 How many ice creams can you see?   ....

LESSON 31

A Find and write

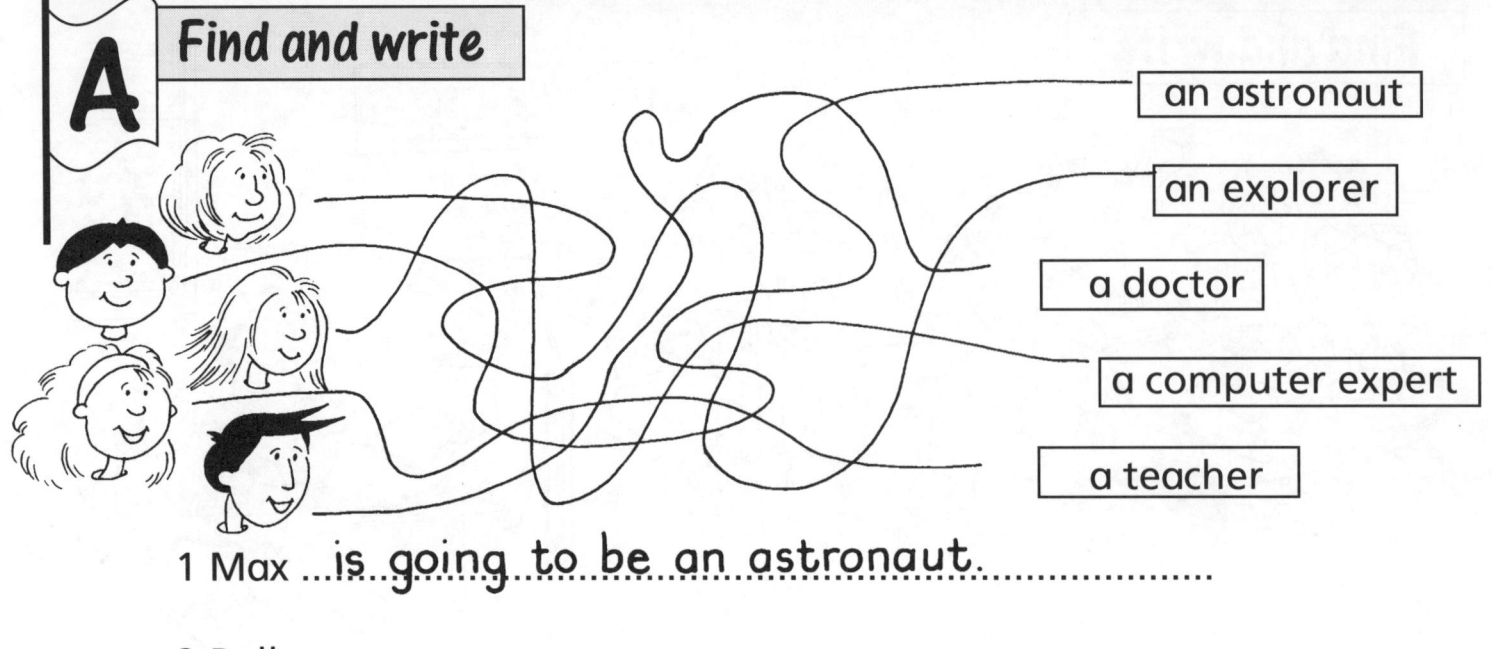

1 Max ...is going to be an astronaut...

2 Polly ....

3 Pete ....

4 Lucy ....

5 Rose ....

B Look and write

Look at Section A.

1 Is Polly going to be a teacher?   Yes, she is..............................

2 Is Max going to be a doctor?   ....

3 Is Pete going to be a teacher?   ....

4 Is Lucy going to be a doctor?   ....

5 Is Rose going to be an explorer? ....

C Look and write

1 Pete ...can swim...
...He can't ski...

2 Polly ....
....

3 Rose ....
....

4 Bob ....
....

These people can ski.
These people can swim.

LESSON 32

A Point, say and write

1 The rubber .... is on the left ....

2 The jumper..............................

3 The pen ....

4 The socks ....

5 The boxes ....

6 The rulers ....

forty three 43

B Choose and write
Look at Section A.

is   are   right   left

1. Where is .... the pen?   It is on the left. ....
2. .... the socks?   ....
3. .... the rulers?   ....
4. .... the boxes?   ....
5. .... the jumper?   ....
6. .... the rubber?   ....

C Look and write

1. She gets up at six o'clock.
2. ....

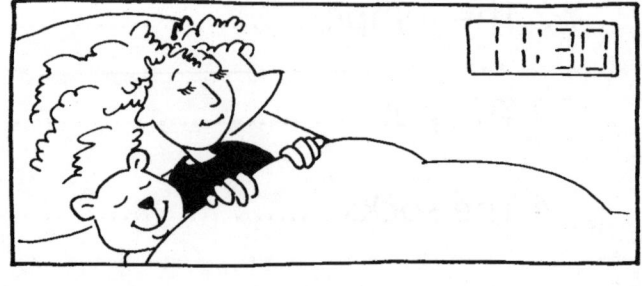

3. ....
4. ....

LESSON 33

A Choose and write

| Pete, Polly and Rose |
| is going to |
| inside   Where's |

Electrobox (1) ...is going to... take off. (2) .... Miss Electra?

Miss Electra is (3) .... Electrobox.

(4) .... aren't inside Electrobox.

B Find and write

1 We're going to eat	..a cake..................	football
2 We're going to do	....	the alphabet
3 We're going to read	....	a song
4 We're going to play	....	our homework
5 We're going to go	....	a kite
6 We're going to make	....	home
7 We're going to feed	....	our books
8 We're going to sing	....	the lions
9 We're going to say	....	a cake

forty-five 45

C Say and write

Winter ....

one ....

....

January ....

....

LESSON 34

A Find and write

eat • bus • desk • red • three • under

bed • key • jumper

B Find and say   Find ten differences.

forty-seven 47

BRAVO! 2 Activity Book
INTERNATIONAL EDITION

Heinemann International
A division of Heinemann Publishers (Oxford) Ltd
Halley Court, Jordan Hill, Oxford, OX2 8EJ

OXFORD LONDON EDINBURGH
MADRID ATHENS BOLOGNA PARIS
MELBOURNE SYDNEY AUCKLAND SINGAPORE TOKYO
IBADAN NAIROBI HARARE GABORONE
PORTSMOUTH (NH)

ISBN 0 435 29194 7

© Judy West C.J. Moore 1993

All rights reserved; no part of this publication may be reproduced, stored
in a retrieval system, or transmitted in any form or by any means,
electronic, mechanical, photocopying, recording, or otherwise,
without the prior written permission of the Publishers.

First published 1993

Designed by Nutshell Design

Illustrated by Lorraine White

Printed and bound in Scotland by Thomson Litho
93 94 95 96 97 98 10 9 8 7 6 5 4 3 2 1